Note for Parents

Crafts and activities are not intended for children under 5 years of age. As with all hands-on craft projects, the activities presented herein require proper adult supervision. Please note that some of the activities depicted in this book include the use of tools and supplies that if misused or used unattended may present a danger to young children. Prior to allowing a child to perform any of the activities in this book, please make sure activities are appropriate for the child's age level.

ISBN: 0-7172-8971-0

Published by Grolier Books, Danbury, CT.

Grolier Books is a division of Grolier Enterprises, Inc.

Produced by J. A. Ball Associates

Designed by Janet Pedersen

Production by Niemand Design

GROLIER
B O O K S

Disney's
Tales of Peace and Joy
with Pooh and Friends
A Timeless Christmas Treasury

By Marc Gave
Art by Kim Raymond

Background Painting by Ruth Blair
Character Inking by John Brown
Activities by Lynn Brunelle
Activities Illustrated by Janet Pedersen

Contents

There's No Christmas Like Snow Christmas

Pooh and Piglet were standing in front of Pooh's front door, bending their necks back as far as they could and staring straight up. The sky looked like a smooth sheet of grey paper stretching out just above the treetops.

Piglet said, almost under his breath, "Pooh, are you thinking what I'm thinking?"

"What are you thinking, Piglet?" Pooh asked. Pooh just happened to be thinking about sitting in an armchair near the fireplace, snacking on honey.

"I'm thinking that there is definitely not a sign of snow," answered Piglet.

"Definitely not," echoed Pooh. "So I think we should go inside and have some honey."

"But Pooh," Piglet pleaded, "if we go inside, how will we know if there's snow on the way?"

"Why do we need to know that?" Pooh asked.

Piglet sighed. "There's always snow at Christmas! If

1

we can't see any snow, then how will Christmas know it's time to come?"

"Oh," replied Pooh. "Oh! This IS a problem. Think, think, think. What to do?"

Finally Pooh had a thought. A very sensible-for-Pooh kind of thought.

"Perhaps, Piglet," he said, "we might ask Owl."

"All right," Piglet agreed.

The two friends started walking to Owl's house. Neither said a word.

Then Piglet broke the silence. "Pooh, I was thinking. What if Owl doesn't know how to make the snow come?"

Pooh scratched his head. "Think, think, think," he told himself. He thought another thought. "Piglet, perhaps if I make up a little hum, the snow will come down to listen."

With that, he began to sing:

Oh, snow way up there in the sky,
Please don't be shy, oh, don't be shy.
Just leave your clouds to come and play,
And make a snowy Christmas Day.

"That was very nice, Pooh," said Piglet admiringly.

Piglet felt a little cheered. But as they walked on, the sky didn't look any different, and they didn't feel a single snowflake.

"I don't mean to complain," continued Piglet, "because it was such a nice hum, Pooh, but there still isn't any snow."

And Pooh couldn't deny that Piglet was right. He spent some more time thinking and then said, "Perhaps if we pretended to be snowflakes and danced the way snowflakes do, real snowflakes would come see what all the dancing was about."

"I—I don't know, Pooh," replied Piglet. "How do snowflakes dance?"

"I'll show you," said Pooh, and he lifted his arms and proceeded to dance this way and that.

As much as Piglet wanted to believe in Pooh, he felt doubtful. There still wasn't any sign of a snowflake, not even one. But there were the sounds of bouncing, and they were coming closer.

Pooh stopped his dancing just as Tigger bounced across the path. "Hello, Pooh! Hello, Piglet!" Tigger exclaimed. "What's up, Buddy Boys?"

"We're going to see Owl," Pooh announced. "Piglet is afraid that if there isn't any snow, Christmas won't know when to come."

"Pooh has already hummed a snow hum and danced a snow dance," explained Piglet. "But it hasn't snowed."

"Hoo-hoo-hoo! This is a serial situation, all right. Very serial. But leave it to Tigger. Getting it to snow is what tiggers do best," Tigger replied.

With that, Tigger bounced into a nearby clearing. "I'll bounce right up into the sky and bring some snow down," he shouted. Then he bounced the highest bounce that Pooh and Piglet had ever seen, and he disappeared right into the sky. Pooh and Piglet waited and waited, but there was no sign of Tigger.

"You don't suppose he got stuck up there, do you, Pooh?" asked Piglet nervously.

"I don't think so," answered Pooh. "Tigger always lands *somewhere*."

Sure enough, when Pooh and Piglet finally reached Owl's house, there was Tigger on the roof. He looked a little crumpled.

"Here I am, Buddy Boys!" called Tigger. "Did you see that bounce? That tiggerific, super-fantastickal bounce?"

"It was very nice, Tigger," said Piglet, "and we thank you for doing it. But I'm afraid it didn't bring any snow."

"Snow? What's this I hear about snow?" asked Owl, coming to his door.

"Well," explained Piglet, "I was telling Pooh that I'm afraid that if there isn't any snow, Christmas won't know when to come. Pooh hummed a hum and danced a dance, but the snow didn't come down. Then Tigger bounced up to take a look and bounce some snow back, but that didn't work either."

Owl looked at them gravely. He was just about to say something when Christopher Robin walked by.

Christopher Robin noticed the long faces on everyone. "Whatever is the matter?" he asked. "Why is everyone so gloomy?"

Pooh told Christopher Robin the whole sad tale.

"Silly old bear," said Christopher Robin when Pooh had finished. He gave Pooh a big hug. "We can't make it

snow just because we want it to."

"We can't?" asked Pooh.

"No," replied Christopher Robin. "It only snows when IT wants to—when everything is a certain way up in the clouds. But Piglet, you don't have to worry. Christmas will come whether there's snow or not.

Christmas knows exactly when to come every year, on December twenty-fifth."

"It does?" asked Piglet. "How clever!"

"It is, indeed," Christopher Robin answered. "In fact, I was just coming to wish everyone a merry Christmas."

"Merry Christmas!" the others shouted, greatly relieved.

"Maybe we should have a Christmas party," suggested Christopher Robin. "A special no-snow Christmas party!"

"I like that idea," said Pooh, clapping his paws. He turned to Owl. "You don't happen to have a smackerel of honey lying around for the party, do you, Owl?"

Owl went to look, and the others followed him inside. They all gathered around the table. "The most important thing about Christmas is being happy together, snow or no snow," Christopher Robin explained.

As the friends began their no-snow party, what do you think happened? Slowly, quietly, because the clouds WERE that certain way Christopher Robin had mentioned, snowflakes began to fall from the sky. And that is how Pooh and Piglet's no-snow party turned into the merriest, happiest SNOW party ever!

Piglet's Snow Globe

"Oh, d-d-dear me," worried Piglet. "There's no snow outside! What shall we do?"

"Don't worry, Piglet," Christopher Robin said, smiling. "We can make it snow inside!"

"Inside?" a puzzled Piglet replied. "How?"

With this homemade snow globe, you can have a blizzard all year round!

WHAT YOU NEED:

- A grown-up (very important!)
- Small, clear glass jar with screw-on lid
- Small plastic figures (trees, a house, a snowman, etc.)
- Strong, waterproof glue
- Water
- 1 drop dishwashing detergent
- 2 tablespoons glitter

WHAT YOU DO:

1 Arrange the plastic figures on the inside of the jar's lid. A grown-up should glue them down for you. Set the lid aside, and let the glue dry for at least an hour.

2 Fill the jar all the way up to the rim with water. Add the drop of dishwashing detergent. Sprinkle in the glitter.

3 When the glue has dried completely, lower the figures into the jar and screw on the lid very tightly. Do this at the sink, because there will be some spilling.

4 The figures will be upside down. Now tip the jar over and give it a little shake. You can have your own magical glitter snowstorm whenever you like!

13

Pooh's Paper Snowstorm

"Oh, bother!" Pooh cried. "I tried to decorate my house with pretty white snow, but somehow it has all disappeared!"

"Silly old bear!" laughed Christopher Robin. "The snow didn't disappear. It melted! But I know how to make snow that won't melt."

After you make this pile of paper snowflakes, hang them from your ceiling, doorway, or anyplace you want a flurry of fun!

WHAT YOU NEED:

- A grown-up (very important!)
- Square pieces of white drawing paper in a variety of sizes (pieces 8 x 8 inches work well)
- Pencil
- Safety scissors
- White thread
- Clear tape

WHAT YOU DO:

1 Fold paper diagonally, like this, to make a triangle.

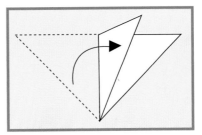

2 Fold the triangle in half by bringing opposite corners together.

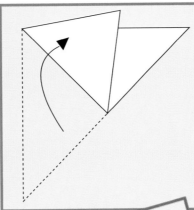

3 Fold the triangle in half again.

4 Draw shapes along the edges of your triangle and cut them out.

5 Gently unfold the triangle and see your beautiful snowflake! Make a pile of snowflakes. Ask a grown-up to help you hang them from the ceiling or doorway with the thread and tape to make a paper snowstorm.

15

Letters to Santa Claus

On the first evening in the month of December, as a full moon shone down brightly on the Hundred-Acre Wood, everyone gathered at Owl's house.

"Hrrumph!" Owl cleared his throat loudly. "This meeting is now about to come to order. The purpose of the meeting, as you all know, is to compose our missives to that noblest of noble personages, that incomparable figure in fur, Mr. Kris Kringle."

"I thought we came so Owl could help us write our letters to Santa Claus," Roo whispered to Kanga.

"Hush, dear," Kanga said gently. "I believe that is what Owl was trying to say."

"Now, then," Owl continued, "in light of my orthographic skills, it is incumbent upon me to craft your simple wishes into monuments of correctness."

"I just wanted him to help me with my spelling," Piglet whispered to Pooh.

"I think that is what Owl means," whispered Kanga, who had overheard Piglet.

17

Everyone except Kanga—who said mothers didn't write to Santa—took a turn with Owl, while the others played quiet games and had some refreshments.

At the end of the evening, all the letters to Santa were finished. Then Owl took them to Christopher Robin, who would put them in an envelope with his own letter to Santa. Before he sent them off, a curious Christopher Robin took a peek at them. He smiled as he fixed the spelling some more, which, despite Owl's best efforts, might have given Santa a rough time.

But there was another problem: Except for Christopher Robin's, not one letter was signed. Owl had forgotten to sign anyone's name—even his own! Can you help Christopher Robin find out whose letter is whose?

Dear Mr. Santa, Sir,

Please don't forget to stop at my house on Christmas Eve, because I am leaving you some special cookies and milk. If it doesn't make your sack too heavy, maybe you can bring me a small gift at the same time. Very small, of course. And only if it's not too much trouble. I could use a new scarf. I like things that are pink and red. Thank you.

To my friend Santa,
My mama says I shouldn't ask for too many things, but that's hard. I'd like a pogo stick, so I can bounce high like Tigger, and a bucket and a shovel, so I can dig in the sand pit, and please bring a pouch warmer for my Mama. It gets cold in there! Is that too many things, Santa? I hope not.
Thank you, Santa.

Dear Santa,

Please bring what I ask for every year—hunny. Hunny is what I like best! If I have enough hunny, I never have to wonder what to have for breakfast. Or lunch. Or dinner. But please be careful, Santa. Watch out for bees. They can make it nasty to sit down for a long time. And Santa, as you know, I keep my hunny in a pot, so please bring it in a pot. Or maybe two or three pots?

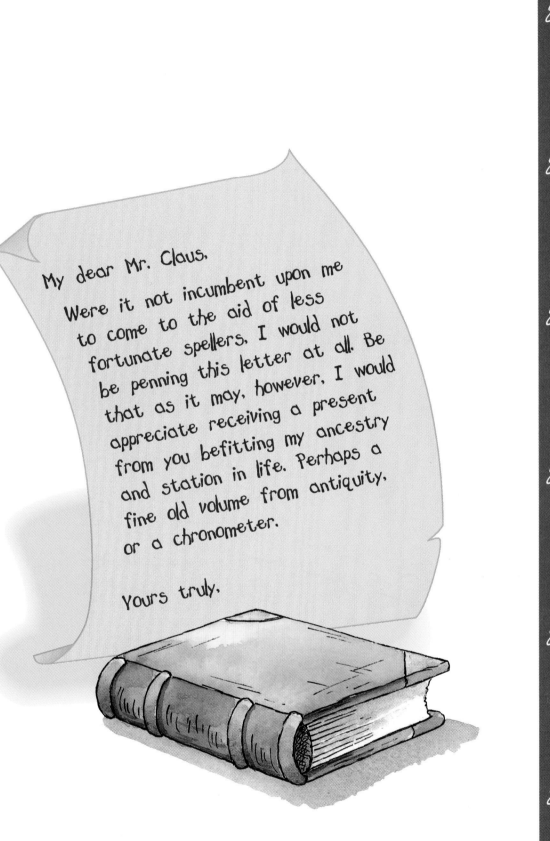

My dear Mr. Claus,

Were it not incumbent upon me to come to the aid of less fortunate spellers, I would not be penning this letter at all. Be that as it may, however, I would appreciate receiving a present from you befitting my ancestry and station in life. Perhaps a fine old volume from antiquity, or a chronometer.

Yours truly,

Dear Santa,

You probably won't even notice where I live, so I almost didn't write, because what's the point, but I got talked into it. So if it isn't too much trouble, I'd appreciate having a pile of sticks so I can fix my house in case it breaks again. But I really don't expect anything.

Your friend anyway,

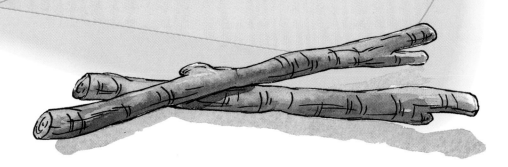

Ho-ho-ho, Santa,

How about a couple of super-big, super-bouncy rubber balls I can bounce around with me on my travels? I had a couple but they bounced out of sight last year. TTFN! Ta-Ta-For-Now, Buddy Boy.

Your friend,

Dear Santa,

Oh, dear, oh, dear, I was almost too busy to write. I had so many turnips and parsnips and kerits and cabeges this year that I ran out of canning jars, so please bring me some more. Also a hat to keep the sun off my head. Don't forget to make holes for my ears.

Hastily,

Dear Santa,

I only want two things, please.
The first is a new sled. The
second is more important: for all
my friends to have a merry
Christmas. Merry Christmas to
you, too, Santa.

Your friend,
Christopher Robin

Pooh's Santa Stationery

"Howdy do, Pooh!" Tigger cried, bouncing his friend to the ground. "What are you doin', pal?"

"Oh, hello, Tigger," Pooh replied from the floor. "Making Santa letters."

"Lucky for you, making letters to Santa is what tiggers do best!" Tigger said. "I'll show you how to make tiggerific stationery! HOO-HOO-HOO-HOO!"

With just an old toothbrush and some paint, you can make your very own splittery, splattery stationery.

WHAT YOU NEED:

- A grown-up (very important!)
- Newspapers to cover your work area
- Smock
- Squares of paper, 4 x 4 inches
- Pencil
- Safety scissors

- Poster paint, nontoxic
- Small pie tin for paint
- Water
- Stick for mixing
- Old toothbrush
- Sheets of white paper, $8\frac{1}{2}$ x 11 inches

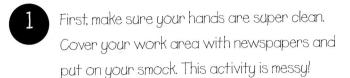

1 First, make sure your hands are super clean. Cover your work area with newspapers and put on your smock. This activity is messy!

2 Using one of the small squares of paper and your pencil, draw a shape. You can make any shape you like.

3 To make a stencil, cut out your shape, leaving the outside portion in one piece.

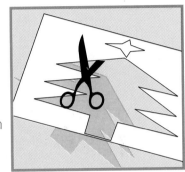

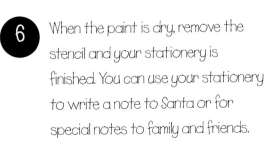

4 Pour paint in the pie tin, add a little water, and mix it thoroughly. Dip your toothbrush in and practice splattering the paint over the newspaper by running your thumb over the bristles.

5 When you've finished practicing, find a clean area of newspaper and set out the white paper. Place your stencil on the paper, at the top or whatever you like. If you want only the shape to show on your stationery, cover the rest of the white pape with scrap paper. Carefully spatter paint on the stencil and let it dry.

6 When the paint is dry, remove the stencil and your stationery is finished. You can use your stationery to write a note to Santa or for special notes to family and friends.

Piglet's Sweets

"C-Christopher Robin!" Piglet cried worriedly. "Since Santa is so busy and I'm so small, do you think he will forget about me?"

"Of course not, Piglet," Christopher Robin replied. "You're much too sweet to forget!"

Here's a little treat that's unforgettably sweet, just like Piglet.

WHAT YOU NEED:

- A grown-up (very important!)
- Roll of prepared refrigerator sugar cookie dough
- Butter or vegetable shortening for greasing pan
- Baking sheet
- Small plastic knife to cut dough
- Container of prepared white icing
- Red food coloring
- Small spatula to mix and spread icing
- Miniature marshmallows
- Miniature chocolate chips

WHAT YOU DO:

1 Slice ¼-inch thick pieces of cookie dough. Place all but four of the slices on a greased baking sheet.

2 Use the extra slices for the following: Cut out small triangles for ears and place two at the top of each round slice as shown. Make small balls of dough and place one in the middle of each round slice. Press it gently into the dough for a nose.

3 A grown-up will turn on the oven and bake the cookies according to directions on the roll. Allow the cookies to cool.

4 Set aside some white icing. In a bowl, mix the remaining icing with one to two drops of the food coloring to make it pink.

5 Ice the entire cookie. Make eyes by placing two marshmallows above the nose. Add chocolate chips for pupils, using a dab of white icing to hold the chips in place.

Enjoy your Piglet-sweet treats! But leave some for Santa!

29

Eeyore's Candy Cane Treasure Hunt

It was the day before Christmas, and Pooh was sitting in his thoughtful spot, humming a little hum. He was trying to think of some words for the hum. But the only thing he could come up with to rhyme with tree was bush. Just then, Eeyore walked by.

"Hello, Eeyore," said Pooh happily. "It's a beautiful day in the Hundred-Acre Wood, isn't it?"

"What's beautiful about it?" asked Eeyore gloomily.

"It's sunny," Pooh explained, "and not too cold, and there's ever so slight a breeze. . . ."

"That will do, Pooh," Eeyore interrupted. "I get the picture."

"But I haven't come to the best part yet," said Pooh insistently. "Today's the day before Christmas."

"So?" replied Eeyore.

"So?" repeated Pooh. "So it's time to celebrate!"

"Oh, you mean all that Christmas stuff," grumbled Eeyore. "That isn't for the likes of me."

Pooh could hardly believe his ears. He was used to

Eeyore being gloomy, but being too gloomy to celebrate at Christmas was . . . well, perhaps the gloomiest he had ever seen Eeyore. And Pooh couldn't bear it.

Then Pooh had a happy thought. "I've got just the thing to cheer you up," he announced. "A Christmas tree."

"Well, maybe," said Eeyore, his voice full of doubt.

"Good," replied Pooh. "First you'll pick out one that you like. Then you'll decorate it. And finally, you'll put presents underneath it."

"Pick one? Decorate? Presents?" asked Eeyore. "I don't think so."

"I'll help you," offered Pooh cheerfully, thinking of

his own tree waiting at home, which was full of decorations he could eat if his tummy got a little empty.

Pooh wouldn't take no for an answer. Once he got an idea in his brain, he didn't like to let it go, in case another one didn't come along.

"Oh, all right," Eeyore agreed reluctantly.

Pooh and Eeyore walked and walked, and Pooh pointed out many a tree that he thought was beautiful. But Eeyore found a problem with each and every tree. It was too large or too small or too handsome for the likes of him. Finally, Eeyore stopped in front of the most pitiful-looking tree Pooh had ever seen.

"This one looks just right to me," said Eeyore.

So Pooh helped Eeyore carry the little tree back to Eeyore's house. Of course, it wouldn't fit inside.

"Oh, well," Eeyore sighed. "Outside's good enough."

They stood the tree next to Eeyore's house. Just then a gust of wind came up and blew the tree away.

"Oh, bother!" exclaimed Pooh.

"Easy come, easy go," Eeyore groaned, thumping down in his little house. "You go off and have your Christmas, Pooh. But it's not meant for the likes of me."

Pooh didn't know what to say. He decided to go home and see if a small smackerel would help him think

34

of a way to make Eeyore less gloomy. On the way he met Kanga and Roo.

"Why, hello, Pooh, dear," greeted Kanga.

"Hi, Pooh!" cried Roo.

"We were just coming to your house to wish you a merry Christmas," Kanga added.

"Thank you, Kanga. Thank you, Roo," replied Pooh. "I have just been to see Eeyore, and for him, it's only another gloomy day. Even the Christmas tree he picked out blew away. Not that it was much of a tree to begin with."

"Oh, dear," Kanga said. "We simply must do something special for poor Eeyore. I will go and tell the others to meet us later to decide on a plan."

That afternoon, just before the sun went down, everyone except Eeyore gathered at Pooh's house. Kanga was carrying a huge basket full of very special things. All the friends talked excitedly, making out the perfect plan.

When Eeyore woke up on Christmas morning, he got a big surprise. Where his tree had been was a shiny new tail ribbon tied around a candy cane.

"What's this?" asked Eeyore.

When he looked around to see if anyone was there, he saw other candy canes hanging on bushes and trees and in the snow. They made a trail leading into the woods.

Eeyore was a little bit curious. "Might as well follow it," he thought. And despite himself, he felt a little bit of his gloominess start to leave him.

He followed the trail, munching candy canes as he
went. The trail ended . . . at Rabbit's house! But
Rabbit's house looked very special this morning. There,
out front, stood a small Christmas tree decorated with
tail ribbons! And under the tree was a neatly wrapped
package.

Eeyore felt the package with his hoof. It was soft and
squishy. He was certain the package was meant for him,
so he opened it. Inside was a small grey pillow with
some writing on it. "Why, if I could read, I might think
that said 'Eeyore,'" he thought.

And there was more. Eeyore followed the next trail of
candy canes to . . . Owl's house!

There he found another Christmas tree decorated
with tail ribbons. Underneath the tree was a bunch of
thistles, tied with a big pink bow. There was still another
trail! Eeyore followed it all the way to . . . Kanga and

Roo's house! All his friends were there, gathered around a beautiful tree. The tree was decorated with tail ribbons and silver snowflakes. And under the tree was a picture frame with a mirror in it. "Now you have enough new tail ribbons to make you feel less gloomy all next year," said Pooh.

"And a mirror so you can see how nice they look," added Piglet, holding up Eeyore's new mirror. The others tied a bunch of ribbons onto Eeyore's tail.

Even Eeyore had to admit he looked like a very handsome donkey.

And Eeyore had to admit something else, too. Inside, where the gloominess usually was, he had a great big happy feeling instead.

"I don't know what to say," Eeyore told everyone. "Except, maybe, thanks."

"Say you won't be gloomy on Christmas," suggested Piglet.

"Well, I don't know about that," said Eeyore slowly.

"Please?" everyone asked at once.

"Oh, all right," agreed Eeyore finally. "Merry Christmas, everyone!"

"Merry Christmas, Eeyore!" all his friends shouted.

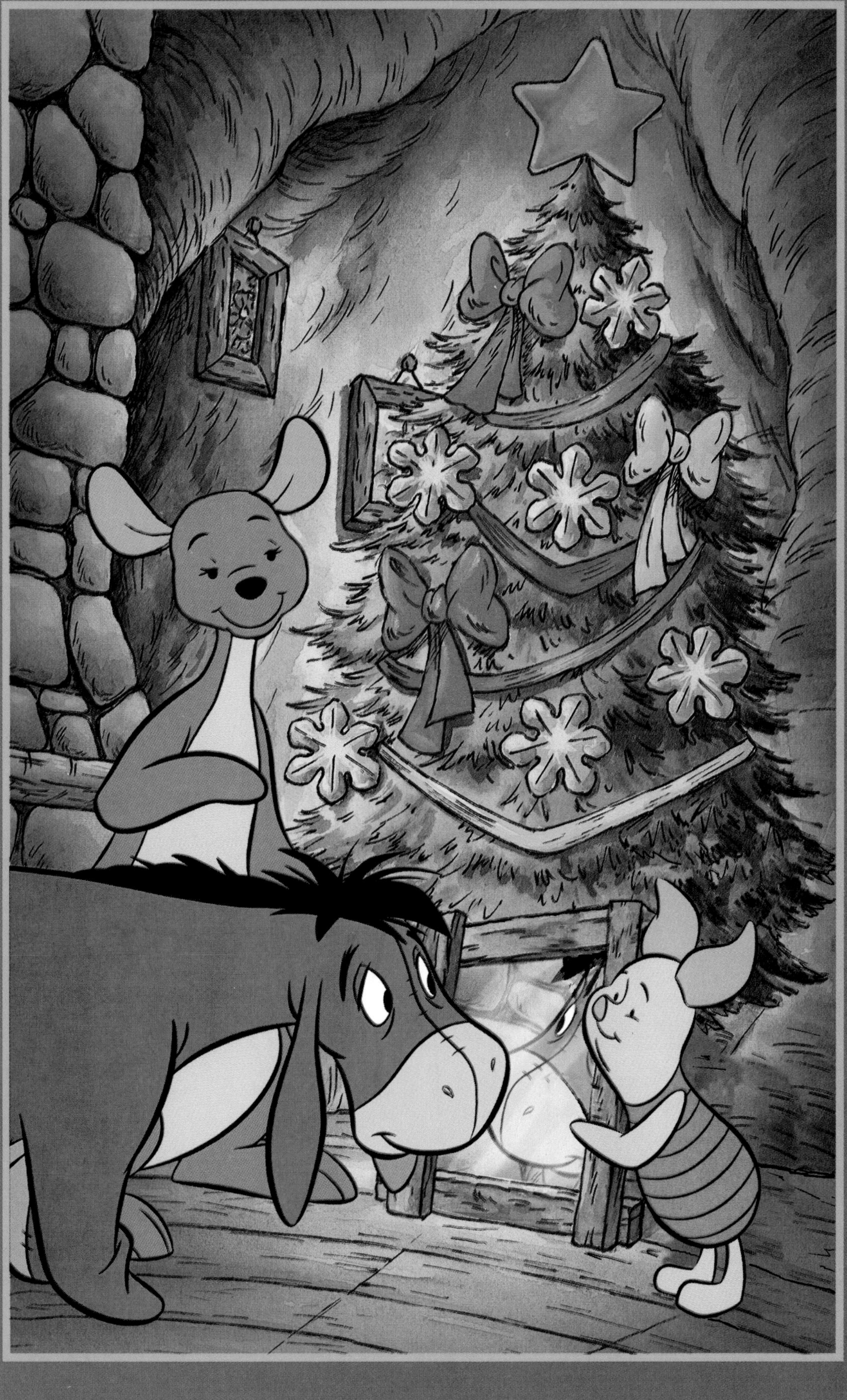

Eeyore's Dough Picture Frame

"No place to hang this picture," grumbled Eeyore. "Oh, well . . ."

"We can make a frame, Eeyore, old pal," Tigger chimed in. "Come on. It'll be fun. We'll make it out of dough."

"Can we eat it?" Pooh asked hopefully.

Here's a dough frame that will make any artwork more special.

WHAT YOU DO:

1 Tape the waxed paper to your work surface. Have a grown-up preheat the oven to 250°F.

2 Prepare the dough: In the bowl, mix the flour and the salt. Gradually add the water. Mix with your hands, kneading the dough until it is smooth.

WHAT YOU NEED:

- A grown-up (very important!)

- Flour dough:
  - 3 cups flour
  - 1 cup salt
  - 1 cup warm water
  - Large bowl
  - Mixing spoon

- Flat work surface
- Waxed paper
- Tape
- Rolling pin
- Ruler
- Toothpick or fork
- Plastic knife

- Pencil
- Baking sheet
- Poster paint, non-toxic
- Water-based glue
- Glitter
- Piece of strong yarn or string

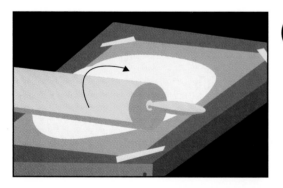

3 Shape the dough into a ball. Place on the waxed paper. Then use a rolling pin to roll out the dough into a flat pancake about 1/4 inch thick.

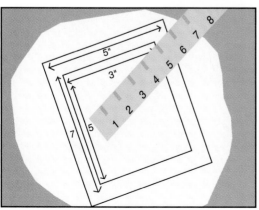

4 In the middle of the pancake, use your ruler to measure out a rectangle 3 x 5 inches. Lightly draw the lines with a toothpick. This will be your inside frame space. Around this rectangle, measure and draw a rectangle 1 inch larger on each side. This larger rectangle (5 x7 inches) will be the outside of the frame.

5

Your grown-up will help you cut along the lines. Peel the extra dough from the middle and around the sides.

6

Use the pencil to make two holes — one in each corner of the top of the rectangle. You'll hang the frame from these holes.

7

Make patterns with the toothpick or the fork to decorate the dough.

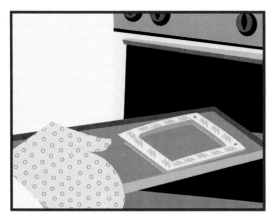

8

Carefully place the dough frame on the baking sheet. Have a grown-up bake the frame for 1 hour, or until golden brown.

9

When it is completely cool, you can decorate your frame with paint or glitter. (For glitter, first apply glue to the frame in a pattern you like.)

10

Glue your artwork to the back of the frame so it shows through the front. Tie the yarn or string through the holes and hang your masterpiece on the wall!

Note: Please do not eat this dough frame.

43

Pin the Star on the Christmas Tree

"I lost my tail again," sighed Eeyore.

"Here it is, Eeyore!" shouted Roo. "May I pin it on?"

Here's a new twist on an old game. Try "taping the star on top of the tree." Sounds easy, but not when you're blindfolded! Other players may help by calling out "jingly" and "jinglier" instead of "warm" and "warmer" when the blindfolded player comes close.

WHAT YOU NEED:

- A grown-up (very important!)
- Safety scissors
- Green construction paper
- White construction paper
- Clear tape
- Blindfold
- Some friends for playing

44

WHAT YOU DO:

1 Have a grown-up help you cut out a tree shape from the green construction paper and hang it on the wall. Each player should be able to reach the top of the tree.

2 Cut out a white star for each player, and ask each player to write his or her name on it.

Pooh

3 Put a folded piece of tape on the back of each star so that some of the sticky side faces out.

4 Players take turns being blindfolded and turned around. Then they're pointed in the direction of the tree. Everyone tries to place a star on the top of the tree. At the end, the person closest to the top wins.

Pooh

Tigger

Piglet

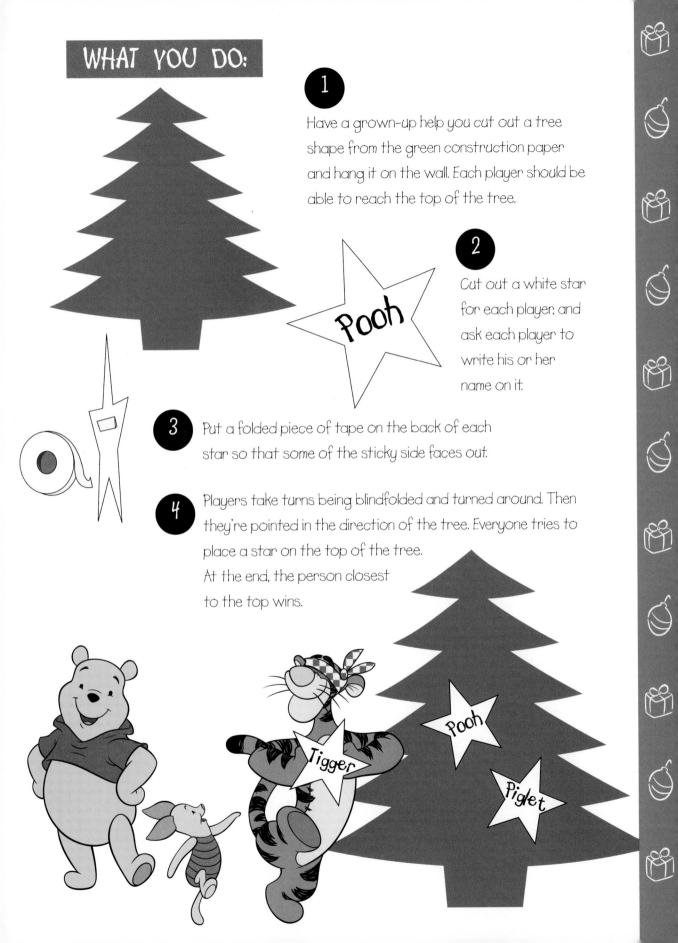

A One-Pooh Open Sled

"Look, Tigger," said Christopher Robin happily on Christmas morning. "Santa brought me just what I asked him for, a new sled."

"Oh boy, oh boy, oh boy!" cried Tigger excitedly. "A new sled! How about that!" Tigger stopped and looked puzzled. He didn't want to admit that he didn't know quite how to use a sled.

"Now, Tigger," began Christopher Robin, "I have to go do something for a while. I'll be back soon. Would you stay here while I'm gone? If any of our friends come by to wish me a merry Christmas, please ask them to stay until I get back. You may play with anything you want—except my new sled."

Tigger agreed. Since he wasn't sure how to use it, he knew he wouldn't be playing with it.

"TTFN—Ta-Ta-For-Now," Tigger shouted after Christopher Robin. "Don't be long."

Christopher Robin was gone only a few moments when Tigger spotted a bit of bright green coming through the woods.

The green spot got bigger . . .

and bigger . . .

. . . and finally Pooh was standing there, a warm green scarf wrapped around where his neck would have been.

"Hello, Tigger," Pooh said.

"Hello, Buddy Bear," replied Tigger. "Christopher Robin will be back soon. . . ."

But Pooh wasn't listening. "What a splendid sled!" Pooh exclaimed. "Oh, Tigger, might we go for a ride until Christopher Robin gets back?"

But Tigger answered, "Sorry. Christopher Robin asked me not to play with the sled while he was gone."

"Oh," sighed Pooh disappointedly. "Well, then, Tigger, perhaps we could just put it down on the snow and get it ready to go for Christopher Robin."

Tigger didn't see how that could do any harm. They put the sled on top of a little hill. Tigger wondered how someone might get it started. Finally his curiosity got the better of him.

"Tell me, Pooh, old Buddy Boy," said Tigger, "what do you have to do to get this thing to move, anyway?"

49

"You just sit down like this," Pooh explained. "And you give a little push with your foot like this, and . . ." Before he knew it, sled and bear were heading down the hill.

"Gosh an' golly!" thought Tigger. "That looks like fun." And without giving it another thought, when Pooh returned to the top of the hill, Tigger asked if he could ride down with him the next time.

"Looks almost as much fun as bouncing," Tigger remarked as he got on behind Pooh. Then Pooh gave a little push with his foot, and they were off, sailing down the hill.

"Hoo-hoo-hoo!" exclaimed Tigger. "Tiggers still like bouncing better than sledding. But tiggers like sledding, too."

"Let's do it again," said Pooh.

But before they had a chance to climb the hill, Piglet appeared in the distance.

"Hello, Pooh. Hello, Tigger," Piglet called, walking toward them. "Merry Christmas. What a beautiful sled!"

"Hop aboard, Piglet Ol' Pal," invited Tigger.

Piglet replied, "I—I don't think there's room for me."

"Oh, stuff and fluff," said Pooh. "There's plenty of room for a very small animal such as yourself. Just climb on behind Tigger."

"Whee!" shouted Piglet as they headed downhill.

But before they got halfway down, the sled overturned, dumping everybody out into the snow.

"S-s-see?" stammered Piglet. "I was right about there not being enough room."

Pooh thought and thought. His thoughts were interrupted by Tigger, who said, "Wait here, Buddy Boys. Tigger has a plan."

He bounced off and was back in a jiffy with a small cardboard box, some rope, and some tape. He taped and tied the box onto the side of the sled. "Now there's room, Piglet," he said proudly.

Piglet looked doubtful, but he got in anyway. The three friends headed down the hill once more. This time they made it all the way down.

"That was fun, Pooh!" cried Piglet. "Let's do it again."

But before they could, Owl appeared. "Never had

much luck with sleds," he remarked. "Or boxes," he added. "They are too—"

"Oh, but we're having so much fun!" interrupted Piglet. "Why don't you join us?"

"There doesn't appear to be enough room," said Owl.

Tigger got another box, which he taped and tied for Owl on the other side of the sled. Down the hill went the four friends.

"Wasn't that fun?" asked Pooh.

"Oh, I suppose," Owl slowly answered, secretly having the time of his life.

Just then Rabbit came along. Tigger set Rabbit up on a frying pan that he tied behind the sled. Soon all were on their way downhill.

As they climbed to the top of the hill once more, they spotted Eeyore in the distance and waved to him to join them.

Eeyore trudged slowly through the snow to the top of the hill. "What do you have there, Pooh?" he asked.

"A sled," replied Pooh. "Isn't it wonderful?"

"It looks more like a sled with two boxes and a frying pan tied on," Eeyore observed.

"That's what I meant," explained Pooh. "It's a special sled. Do you want to come sledding, too? There's room for a fine seat for you right in the front."

"Oh, that would be too good for the likes of me," replied Eeyore.

But Pooh insisted, and Tigger went off again and returned with a large washbowl, which he tied to the front.

"Well, here we go!" he shouted.

But the sled got stuck halfway down the hill.

Just then they saw Christopher Robin passing by. And Christopher Robin saw the sledding party stuck on the hill.

"Uh-oh," gulped Pooh, suddenly remembering that they weren't supposed to be playing with Christopher Robin's sled.

But Christopher Robin took one look at the sled with the boxes, the frying pan, the washbowl, and the friends stuck on the hill, and he burst out laughing. He laughed so hard that he almost fell down into the snow.

"You're not angry?" asked Pooh.

Christopher Robin didn't answer him but said, "Well, Tigger, what do you have to say for yourself?"

"It wasn't Tigger's fault," replied Pooh. "It was mine. I'm sorry."

"Apology accepted. And I'm not angry." Christopher Robin smiled. "You gave me such a good laugh, how can I be angry? I would have let all of you use my new sled anyhow. I just wanted to take the first ride."

Everyone sang a chorus of "For He's a Jolly Good Fellow" to Christopher Robin. Then Christopher Robin tied some more rope around the washbowl and pulled everyone out of the snowbank.

"Come, let's all get some hot chocolate," Christopher Robin suggested. "Then we can do some more sledding—but perhaps not everybody at the same time!"

Kanga's Perfect Popcorn Pals

"Oh, Kanga," Pooh asked, smacking his lips, "is that honey I see on the counter?"

"Yes, Pooh, dear," replied Kanga. "I'll be adding this honey to popcorn to make a special Christmas treat."

"Hmm," said Pooh. "I wonder, Kanga, if I may have my treat without the fuss of popcorn?"

Here are some delicious snow pals that your mouth will be happy to make friends with!

WHAT YOU NEED:

- A grown-up (very important!)
- Large mixing bowl
- 10 cups popped popcorn
- Medium saucepan
- 1 cup confectioners' sugar
- $1/4$ teaspoon cinnamon
- $1/2$ cup honey
- 4 tablespoons butter
- 2 tablespoons water

- 2 teaspoons vanilla
- 1 cup squished marshmallows (squish them into the cup tightly)
- 2 large cooking spoons
- Softened butter or margarine for greasing hands
- Extra honey for forming snow friends
- Waxed paper
- Gumdrops or other small candies for decoration

WHAT YOU DO:

1

Place the popped popcorn in the mixing bowl.

2

To make a syrup, place the sugar, cinnamon, honey, butter, water, vanilla, and marshmallows in the saucepan. A grown-up should heat the mixture over low heat, stirring constantly until the marshmallows melt and the syrup begins to boil.

3 A grown-up should pour the hot syrup over the popcorn and use two large cooking spoons to toss it well until all the popcorn is coated. Then leave the popcorn to cool a bit.

4 When the grown-up says that the popcorn is cool enough, wash your hands. Then grease your hands with a little softened butter or margarine, dip them into the popcorn, and — one at a time — form popcorn balls. Shape snow friends from the balls, sticking parts together with extra honey. Set them on waxed paper. Decorate by making eyes, nose, and mouth out of candy. Let them sit for about an hour, or until they are hard. Enjoy!

Christopher Robin's Tummy-Warming Punch

"Here, Pooh, try some tummy-warming punch," Christopher Robin said.

"But Christopher Robin," Pooh asked puzzledly, "how can your warm drink punch my tummy?"

"Silly old bear!" Christopher Robin laughed. "Punch is another name for a fruit juice drink!"

Here's a fun treat that will add punch to any holiday party!

WHAT YOU NEED:

- A grown-up (very important!)
- 4 cups cranberry juice drink
- 2 cups orange juice
- 10 cloves
- 3 cinnamon sticks
- 6 orange slices, about $1/4$ inch thick
- 1 teaspoon honey
- Saucepan, at least 2-quart size
- Strainer
- Mugs

WHAT YOU DO:

1 Place the juices, spices, oranges, and honey in a saucepan.

2 Have a grown-up help you heat the mixture and let it simmer, covered, for 20 minutes.

3 Have your grown-up strain the spices out and pour the mixture into mugs. Let the mixture cool down a bit before drinking.

4 Enjoy sipping this warm punch after sledding.

The Hundred-Acre Wood Wintry Alphabet

A is for Angels you make in the snow.

B is for Baking treats made from sweet dough.

C is for Candles so bright in their holders.

D is for Drifts of snow up to your shoulders.

E is for Eeyore, who always looks sad.

F is for Friends— when you see them, you're glad.

64

G is for Games to be played without haste.

H is for Honey
so sweet to the taste.

I is for Ice skates to
glide on the ice.

J is for Jingle bells
sounding so nice.

K is for Kanga,
little Roo's
caring mother.

L is for Love,
which they feel
for each other.

M is for Moonlight
that lights up the snow.

66

N is for Neighbors, who wave as you go.

O is for Owl, who talks on without end.

P is for Piglet, Pooh's good-natured friend.

Q is for Quilt, which keeps cold winds away.

R is for Rabbit, who works night and day.

S is for Smackerel, just a wee bite.

T is for Tigger, who bounced out of sight.

U is for Up,
a long way
from below.

V is for Vegetables
Rabbit helps grow.

W is for Wood, which you
walk through with pleasure.

X marks the spot where you find buried treasure.

Y is for Yule log. Mmm! What a good sight!

Z is for Zzz's while you sleep through the night.

Owl's New Year's Resolutions

It had been a wonderful Christmas in the Hundred-Acre Wood. There was plenty of snow. Santa arrived right on time and brought everyone what they wanted. There were lots of other presents exchanged, too, and good food, indoor games, and outdoor fun. Best of all, there was the great feeling of peace and joy that comes from true friendship.

But that wasn't enough for Owl. He had a nagging feeling that somehow he was forgetting to do something important. He went fussing and fuming all over the house, and the day before New Year's, he finally realized what it was: It was the time of year when you decide how to make things better!

So Owl called a meeting at Pooh's house, saying he had something important to share with all of his friends. Christopher Robin was away on a trip, and Kanga and Roo couldn't come, but everyone else was there.

"I thank you for coming," Owl began. "In the past

week we have all had a wonderful time celebrating. Now, with the New Year upon us, it is time for some thinking, rumination, and reflection. There is an ancient, well-founded, and long-standing custom that is just the tonic . . ."

"Owl," Rabbit interrupted, "could you please get to the point? Some of us have work to do."

"The point is that each of us could be better than we are, and that's why we should each make a New Year's resolution," Owl summed up.

"Why didn't you say so in the first place?" Rabbit asked impatiently.

There was silence in the room as Rabbit looked around. Finally he said, "Wellll, I suppose I could try to be less impatient."

"That's the spirit," replied Owl.

Tigger, still feeling the effects of bouncing after eating Christmas treats, added, "I guess I could bounce less."

Pooh, getting carried away in the moment, blurted out, "I will try to eat less honey next year." Then, realizing what he had said, he patted his tummy a bit sadly.

Eeyore announced he would try to be less gloomy, but he immediately began to worry that he couldn't.

Piglet thought and thought about what he could do less—or more—of. Finally he said, "I'll try not to get lonely or frightened so often, and I won't insist so much on having company."

75

As the meeting was breaking up and Rabbit was
halfway out the door, he suddenly stopped. "What about
you, Owl? What's your resolution?"

Owl, for once, was speechless. "Um . . . er . . . ,"
he sputtered.

"I have one," offered Rabbit. "How about if you use
shorter words?"

Before Owl could protest, Rabbit was gone.

During the next week, the Hundred-Acre Wood was full of resolutions being followed. When Christopher Robin returned home, he decided to call on his friends, stopping by Pooh's house one morning at eleven. Pooh didn't once mention honey. He also didn't seem to be his usual cheerful self. Christopher Robin didn't know what was wrong. Thinking it might cheer Pooh up, he asked, "Isn't it time for a smackerel, Pooh Bear?"

Pooh sighed and said, "I think I will wait until lunchtime."

Puzzled, Christopher Robin said good-bye and headed for Piglet's house. Piglet was waiting at the door.

"Hello, Piglet," Christopher Robin began.

"Hello to you, too, Christopher Robin," replied Piglet. "Well, it's been nice seeing you. So long."

Again, Christopher Robin was puzzled. Usually Piglet loved it when Christopher Robin came to visit, especially when he had been away from the Hundred-Acre Wood for a while.

Next, Christopher Robin went to Rabbit's. "Well, hello, Christopher Robin," Rabbit said, stopping his work. He sat and talked about the weather for a half-hour. It wasn't like Rabbit to sit still for so long. Finally Christopher Robin excused himself.

Next he visited Eeyore. "Well, hello, Christopher Robin!" exclaimed Eeyore brightly. "It's great to see you again." Christopher Robin had never seen Eeyore so cheerful.

He was beginning to wonder if he had come home to the right Hundred-Acre Wood.

On the way back from Eeyore's, Tigger came walking out slowly—not bouncing—from behind some trees.

"Now I know something is wrong," said Christopher Robin. "What happened to your bounce, Tigger?"

"Well, Buddy Boy, it's my New Year's restitution," answered Tigger.

"You mean resolution," Christopher Robin corrected. "Aha! So that's what's the matter with everybody. Tigger, whose idea was it to make these resolutions?"

"Owl!" he blurted out. "Exactickally one week ago."

"I should have known," chuckled Christopher Robin.

"Oh, but we all made our own restitutions," Tigger added.

"Resolutions can be good," explained Christopher Robin, "but not if it changes you too much. I miss my old friends, and I want them back. I think it's time for Owl to call another meeting."

Which is exactly what Owl did. Christopher Robin told everyone what he had said to Tigger. Everybody was happy that they could stop following their resolutions.

Pooh spoke up. "My tummy has been rumbly for days. When I get home, I'm going to have a whole big pot of honey. Well, maybe I could leave some in the pot. I know—that can be my resolution! I'll just eat a little bit less at each meal."

Next, Piglet announced that Christopher Robin could visit for as long as he wanted to whenever he wanted to, as long as it wasn't a bother.

"You're not a bother to me, Piglet," replied Christopher Robin. "And if you ever are, I will tell you. That way you won't have to worry that you are being a bother. And if I am ever being a bother to you, please tell me."

"I will," agreed Piglet.

Next, Rabbit breathed a sigh of relief that he could go back and work all he wanted. "But," he said, "maybe I should take a little time off once in a while, especially when you come by, Christopher Robin."

Eeyore admitted that trying to be cheerful was . . . well, trying. But he thought that maybe he could have one cheerful hour every month.

And Tigger promised to put the bounce back in his step, although maybe he could bounce a little less around Rabbit.

As for Owl, he had tried to give up long words, but hadn't succeeded—not one bit.

"Now, that's more like the Hundred-Acre Wood I know," declared Christopher Robin.

And everybody was happy—well, not exactly everybody. Eeyore was his gloomy old self again. But that was the way it was supposed to be.

Nifty New Year's Hats

"It's New Year's Eve and we have no hats," grumbled Rabbit.

"We may not have hats right now, Rabbit," said Christopher Robin, picking up a brown paper bag. "But we can make them!"

Here are some wild hats made out of paper bags. They're sure to make any celebration a happy one.

WHAT YOU NEED:

- A grown-up (very important!)
- Paper grocery bags
- Poster paint
- Paint brushes
- Wrapping paper
- Tape
- Water-based glue
- Glitter
- Curly ribbon

1

Roll up the edges of a grocery bag until you have an opening that fits your head. If it won't stay rolled up, tape it. Shape the rest of the bag just the way you like.

2

Decorate the bag with paint— have fun! Tape strips of shiny wrapping paper on the rim. Use glue and glitter to write your name on the front. Hang loads of curly ribbon from the top. Do whatever else you think will make it nice! Let your hat dry. When it's dry, put it on and ring in the New Year with style!

83

Good Old Friends

(Melody: "Auld Lang Syne")

Should Pooh see Piglet strolling by
In the Hundred-Acre Wood,
Should Owl meet Tigger bouncing up,
In his leafy neighborhood,
They'd say "How do you do, old chum?"
And "Please, why not come in?"
For that's how friends greet friends, you see,
And how it's always been.

Should Kanga, Roo, and Rabbit, too,
All show up at Eeyore's place,
He'd come outside to welcome them.
In his house he has no space.
And no one's ever turned away
From Christopher Robin's door.
For that's how friends treat friends, you see,
For now and evermore.

84